Title:

"Projection to Empowerment: A Comprehensive Guide to Unveiling and Healing Psychological Projections Using Pendulum Therapy"

Introduction

Within the intricate weave of the human mind's tapestry, projections emerge as elusive veils, casting shadows over our authentic selves and distorting the lens through which we perceive the world. "Projection to Empowerment" navigates the depths of psychology, unravelling the enigmatic nature of projections and introducing remedial transformations through the time-honoured practice of Pendulum Healing.

In the complex landscape of human consciousness, projections serve as nuanced layers, concealing the essence of our true selves and skewing the clarity of our perceptions. This exploration into psychology's profound dimensions forms the essence of "Projection to Empowerment," a journey that peels back the layers of projection mysteries. It illuminates the transformative potential inherent in Pendulum Healing, an ancient art that holds keys to restoring balance and unveiling authenticity.

What are "projections"?

In psychology, "projections" refer to a defence mechanism where individuals attribute their own thoughts, feelings, or characteristics onto someone else. This process often involves unconsciously ascribing one's own traits, desires, or emotions to others, externalizing internal conflicts, and perceiving them as originating from external sources. Projections can manifest in various forms, such as projecting insecurities, fears, or unresolved issues onto other people or situations.

For example, an individual who struggles with feelings of inadequacy might project those feelings onto a colleague, perceiving the colleague as judgmental or critical. In reality, these judgments are a reflection of the individual's own internal struggles rather than an accurate assessment of the colleague's behaviour.

Understanding projections is crucial in psychology because it provides insights into an individual's unconscious processes and can be a gateway to self-discovery and personal growth. Recognizing and addressing projections can contribute to improved interpersonal relationships, emotional well-being, and a deeper understanding of one's own psyche.

Chapter 1:

Unveiling the Shadows

This chapter lays the groundwork by exploring the concept of psychological projections. Readers gain insights into how unconscious thoughts, feelings, and aspects of the self are projected onto others, shaping our perceptions and interactions. The pendulum becomes a metaphorical lantern, guiding individuals through the shadows of their own psyche.

"Unveiling the Shadows" is a metaphorical journey into the depths of the human psyche, an exploration that involves bringing to light the concealed aspects of the self. In the context of psychology, this phrase suggests the process of uncovering and understanding the hidden or unconscious elements that influence thoughts, emotions, and behaviors.

This journey involves shining a light on the shadows – the parts of ourselves that we may not readily acknowledge or are not fully aware of. It encompasses self-reflection, introspection, and a willingness to confront aspects of the mind that might be obscured or obscured by defense mechanisms.

"Unveiling the Shadows" is an invitation to delve into the intricacies of one's own consciousness, to illuminate the darker corners where fears, desires, and unresolved issues may reside. It's a step towards self-awareness and self-discovery, recognizing that by acknowledging and understanding these hidden aspects, individuals can gain greater control over their lives and foster personal growth.

Chapter 2:

The Dance of Energy

Delving into the energetic dynamics of projections, this chapter introduces the idea that these psychological phenomena are intertwined with the subtle energies that govern our existence. The pendulum, as an energy interpreter, helps readers understand the vibrational dance between projections and the broader energetic field.

The Dance of Energy" invokes a metaphorical exploration into the dynamic interplay of subtle forces that shape the human experience. In the context of psychological and spiritual realms, this phrase signifies an intricate choreography of energies that influence thoughts, emotions, and actions.

This dance involves understanding the energetic currents that flow within and around individuals, acknowledging the interconnectedness of mind, body, and spirit. It suggests a recognition that thoughts and emotions carry an energetic vibration, creating a ripple effect that extends beyond the individual.

"The Dance of Energy" encourages an awareness of how personal energies interact with the energies of the surrounding environment, as well as with the energies of other individuals. It hints at the idea that cultivating positive energy within oneself can contribute to a harmonious dance with the energies of the external world.

This metaphorical dance underscores the importance of balance, alignment, and attunement to the subtle energies that influence well-being. Exploring this dance invites individuals to become conscious participants in the energetic ebb and flow of life, fostering a deeper understanding of the interconnected forces that shape their experiences.

"The Dance of Energy" involves delving into practical applications and understanding how this metaphorical dance manifests in various aspects of life:

Energetic Self-Reflection:

Individuals are encouraged to engage in self-reflection to discern their own energetic patterns. This may involve exploring how thoughts, emotions, and actions contribute to the overall energetic dance within themselves.

Interpersonal Dynamics:

The dance extends beyond the individual to interpersonal relationships. Recognizing the interplay of energies in relationships allows for a more conscious and harmonious interaction with others.

Mind-Body Connection:

Exploring the mind-body connection is integral to understanding the dance of energy. Practices such as meditation, yoga, or breathwork become tools for attuning the body's energy to the rhythm of the mind and spirit.

Environmental Influence:

The environment plays a role in this dance as well. Awareness of how external factors, such as nature, surroundings, or even cultural influences, impact personal energy adds another layer to the exploration.

Energetic Alignment:

Striving for alignment involves consciously choosing thoughts, emotions, and actions that resonate with one's authentic self. This alignment contributes to a smoother and more positive dance of energy in various life situations.

Energy Transmutation:

Transforming negative or stagnant energies into positive ones is a key aspect of the dance. Techniques such as mindfulness, gratitude practices, or energy healing modalities become tools for transmuting and elevating energies.

Intuitive Guidance:

Trusting one's intuition becomes an integral part of navigating the dance of energy. Tuning into inner wisdom helps individuals make decisions and take actions that are in harmony with their energetic flow.

Cyclical Nature:

Recognizing the cyclical nature of energy allows individuals to navigate life's ups and downs with resilience. Understanding that energy, like a dance, has its rhythms and seasons, fosters a more balanced and patient approach.

By continuing the exploration of "The Dance of Energy," individuals embark on a journey of self-discovery, aligning with the natural rhythms of existence. It involves embracing the interconnectedness of internal and external energies, fostering a conscious and intentional dance that contributes to overall well-being and personal growth.

Chapter 3:

Pendulum Therapy

Readers are introduced to the fundamentals of Pendulum Therapy as a powerful tool for unravelling and healing projections. This chapter explains the mechanics of pendulum movements and how they serve as conduits for accessing the subconscious mind. Practical exercises offer hands-on experience in working with the pendulum for self-discovery.

Exploring the Depths of Pendulum Therapy:

In this transformative chapter, "Pendulum Therapy," readers are immersed in the profound world of Pendulum Therapy—a modality that transcends the ordinary and unveils the extraordinary potential within the human psyche.

Fundamentals of Pendulum Movements:

The chapter commences by demystifying the fundamentals of Pendulum Therapy, providing a lucid understanding of the mechanics behind pendulum movements. Readers gain insights into the subtle dynamics that govern the pendulum's responses, unravelling the mystery of its delicate sways and rotations.

Conduits to the Subconscious Mind:

Central to this exploration is the revelation of how pendulum movements serve as conduits to the subconscious mind. The chapter illuminates the intricate relationship between the conscious and subconscious realms, explaining how the pendulum becomes a bridge that accesses the reservoir of thoughts, emotions, and memories lying beneath the surface.

Practical Exercises for Self-Discovery:

Guiding readers through hands-on experiences, practical exercises unfold the art of working with the pendulum for self-discovery. These exercises empower individuals to pose questions that unravel the layers of the subconscious, offering profound insights into their inner landscapes.

Unlocking Hidden Realms:

As readers engage in Pendulum Therapy exercises, they embark on a journey of unlocking hidden realms within themselves. The pendulum becomes a key, opening doors to self-awareness and unveiling aspects of the psyche that may have remained obscured or unexplored.

Healing Projections Through Pendulum Insights:

The chapter emphasizes the therapeutic potential of Pendulum Therapy in unravelling and healing projections. By understanding the mechanics of the pendulum, readers are equipped to navigate the complexities of projections—those veils that obscure true selves. The pendulum, in this context, becomes a trusted guide in the journey toward self-empowerment and healing.

A Subconscious Symphony:

Immersing deeper into Pendulum Therapy, readers discover that the movements of the pendulum orchestrate a subconscious symphony. The subtle vibrations and oscillations become notes in a melody that harmonizes conscious and unconscious aspects, fostering a holistic and integrated approach to self-discovery and healing.

Cultivating Intuition and Trust:

The chapter concludes by nurturing the development of intuition and trust in the Pendulum Therapy process. Readers are encouraged to cultivate a symbiotic relationship with the pendulum, recognizing it not only as a tool but as a collaborator in their journey towards self-unveiling and healing.

In "Pendulum Therapy," readers are not merely spectators; they are active participants in a transformative experience. This chapter serves as a gateway, opening doors to the profound potentials of Pendulum Therapy, offering a glimpse into the intricate mechanics that make it a powerful tool for self-discovery and healing.

Chapter 4:

Identifying Personal Projections

Guided by the pendulum's wisdom, individuals learn to identify and acknowledge their own projections. The chapter provides insights into posing targeted questions to reveal hidden aspects of the self-projected onto others. The pendulum becomes a truth-seeker, aiding individuals in recognizing and owning their projections.

Unmasking the Veiled Reflections:

As the journey through the realms of self-discovery continues, "Identifying Personal Projections" emerges as a pivotal chapter, inviting readers to unmask the veiled reflections that shape their perceptions and interactions.

The Mirror Within:

Readers delve into the reflective nature of personal projections, understanding that the external world often serves as a mirror reflecting internal thoughts, emotions, and unresolved aspects. The chapter encourages introspection, prompting individuals to scrutinize the reflections cast upon their relationships and experiences.

Guided Queries with the Pendulum:

The pendulum takes center stage as a guide through the process of identifying personal projections. Readers are introduced to targeted questions designed to unveil hidden beliefs, fears, and desires projected onto others. The pendulum becomes a dynamic instrument for self-inquiry, providing nuanced responses that reveal the intricacies of the internal landscape.

Recognizing Patterns and Themes:

The chapter unravels the idea that personal projections manifest as recurring patterns and themes in relationships and daily encounters. Readers learn to discern these patterns, recognizing that they are not arbitrary but rooted in deeper aspects of the self. The pendulum becomes a tool for pattern recognition, assisting individuals in deciphering the symbolic language of their projections.

Ownership and Accountability:

A central theme emerges around ownership and accountability. The chapter emphasizes the empowering act of taking responsibility for one's projections, acknowledging that they are a product of individual perceptions. The pendulum serves as a mirror, reflecting not only projections but also the agency to transform and transcend them.

Shedding Light on Unconscious Motivations:

Readers gain insights into the unconscious motivations that drive personal projections. The pendulum becomes a lantern, illuminating the shadows of the psyche and bringing to light the motives and desires that may be hidden from conscious awareness. This newfound awareness becomes a catalyst for personal growth and transformation.

Healing Through Awareness:

The chapter concludes with a focus on healing through awareness. By identifying personal projections, individuals embark on a journey of self-healing. The pendulum, as a beacon of insight, guides readers in navigating the path toward greater self-awareness and fostering healthier, more authentic relationships.

Integration with Pendulum Commands:

The integration of Pendulum Commands is introduced as a complementary aspect, allowing readers to use the pendulum not only for identification but also for initiating transformative commands that dissolve limiting projections. This integration forms a holistic approach to addressing and evolving beyond personal projections.

In "Identifying Personal Projections," readers traverse the fascinating terrain of self-reflection, guided by the wisdom of the pendulum. The chapter stands as an invitation to confront the veiled aspects of the self, fostering a journey towards profound self-awareness and personal liberation.

The Pendulum as a Truth-Seeker:

The narrative unfolds as the pendulum assumes the role of a truth-seeker, helping individuals unravel the intricacies of their projections. Each swing and oscillation becomes a dialogue with the subconscious, uncovering layers of beliefs and emotions that might have been concealed.

Interactive Exercises for Insight:

Practical exercises within this chapter foster an interactive engagement with the pendulum. Readers are encouraged to participate actively, posing questions that target specific areas of their lives where projections may be at play. This hands-on approach ensures a personalized and insightful exploration.

Navigating the Emotional Landscape:

The emotional landscape is a focal point as readers learn to navigate the terrain of their feelings. The pendulum becomes a compass, pointing towards unresolved emotions and unexplored facets of the self. This navigation is not only a process of discovery but a transformative journey towards emotional intelligence.

Harmony Through Self-Discovery:

By identifying personal projections, readers are on a quest for harmony within themselves and their relationships. The pendulum's revelations become a melody of self-discovery, guiding individuals to harmonize their internal dynamics and foster a more balanced and authentic connection with the world.

Empowerment Through Self-Ownership:

Ownership of personal projections emerges as an empowering theme. The pendulum encourages readers to embrace these projections not with judgment but with a compassionate understanding. Recognizing projections becomes a stepping stone to reclaiming personal power and agency.

Symbols and Metaphors Unveiled:

Symbols and metaphors embedded within projections are unveiled. The pendulum, acting as an interpreter, assists individuals in deciphering the symbolic language of the subconscious. Through this process, projections cease to be mere distortions; they become messages, guiding individuals towards deeper self-awareness.

Integration of Insights into Daily Life:

The chapter seamlessly guides readers in integrating newfound insights into their daily lives. The pendulum transitions from a tool used in specific exercises to a constant companion, offering guidance in real-time situations. This integration fosters a continuous and transformative relationship with personal projections.

A Holistic Approach to Healing:

Healing is presented as a holistic endeavor. By identifying and understanding personal projections, individuals embark on a journey towards holistic well-being. The pendulum, as a facilitator of this journey, supports the integration of insights into daily practices, fostering lasting transformation.

Moving Beyond Limitations:

As the chapter concludes, the pendulum becomes a symbol of moving beyond limitations. It signifies not only the identification of projections but the dynamic process of growth and evolution. Readers are encouraged to view the pendulum as a partner in the ongoing dance of self-discovery.

"In Identifying Personal Projections," readers emerge not only with a heightened awareness of their projections but with a profound sense of agency. The pendulum, as a guide through this unveiling process, invites individuals to step into their own narrative, acknowledging projections as opportunities for growth, healing, and the continuous unfoldment of the authentic self.

Chapter 5:

Remedies Through Pendulum Commands

This pivotal chapter explores the therapeutic potential of Pendulum Commands for healing projections. Readers discover specific commands and affirmations designed to dissolve projection patterns and promote self-awareness. The pendulum transforms into a healing wand, facilitating the release of ingrained projections and fostering personal empowerment.

Harnessing the Healing Power:

Embarking on a transformative journey, "Remedies Through Pendulum Commands" unveils the potency of using intentional commands to dissolve and heal projections. This chapter serves as a guide to harnessing the healing power within the rhythmic swings of the pendulum.

The Art of Pendulum Commands:

Readers are initiated into the art of crafting Pendulum Commands — purposeful statements designed to evoke positive change. This section demystifies the process, outlining the elements of effective commands and offering examples tailored to address various aspects of projection-related challenges.

Affirmative Transformations:

Pendulum Commands become vehicles for affirmative transformations. Readers discover how intentional language, infused with positive energy, can rewire subconscious patterns. The pendulum becomes an active participant in this alchemical process, amplifying the resonance of healing affirmations.

Dissolving Limiting Beliefs:

The chapter delves into how Pendulum Commands can specifically target and dissolve limiting beliefs embedded in projections. By posing commands aimed at restructuring thought patterns, individuals embark on a journey of dismantling self-imposed barriers and embracing empowering narratives.

Navigating Emotional Residue:

Pendulum Commands are revealed as effective tools for navigating emotional residue tied to projections. The chapter provides a nuanced approach, guiding readers to formulate commands that address unresolved emotions. The pendulum becomes a conduit for emotional release and restoration.

Cultivating Positive Self-Image:

Readers are encouraged to use Pendulum Commands to cultivate a positive self-image. The pendulum serves as a mirror, reflecting back affirmations that counteract negative self-perceptions rooted in projections. This practice becomes a transformative ritual for fostering self-love and acceptance.

Healing Relationships Through Commands:

The application of Pendulum Commands extends to healing relationships affected by projections. Readers explore how commands can be directed towards fostering understanding, communication, and harmony. The pendulum becomes a mediator, facilitating a shift in the energetic dynamics of interpersonal connections.

Guided Exercises for Empowerment:

Practical exercises guide readers through the process of crafting and employing Pendulum Commands. These hands-on activities offer a tangible experience of the healing potential embedded in intentional language. The pendulum, as a responsive ally, becomes a tool for personal empowerment.

Integration of Commands into Daily Practice:

"Remedies Through Pendulum Commands" emphasizes the integration of this healing modality into daily life. Readers learn to seamlessly incorporate Pendulum Commands into their routines, establishing a continuous dialogue with the pendulum for ongoing support and transformation.

Empowering Self-Healing:

The chapter concludes by reinforcing the notion that Pendulum Commands empower self-healing. By mastering this art, individuals not only dissolve projections but actively participate in their own healing journey. The pendulum becomes a symbol of agency and a catalyst for sustained personal growth.

In "Remedies Through Pendulum Commands," readers are equipped with a transformative tool for conscious healing. This chapter invites individuals to harness the dynamic energy of intentional commands, allowing the pendulum to guide them through a process of profound self-empowerment and projection dissolution.

The Pendulum as a Catalyst:

Within the realm of Pendulum Commands, the pendulum assumes the role of a catalyst for change. Each swing becomes a conduit for transformative energy, amplifying the resonance of intentional commands that reverberate through the subconscious.

Crafting Personalized Commands:

Readers are encouraged to personalize Pendulum Commands, infusing them with sincerity and relevance to their unique experiences. The chapter provides guidance on tailoring commands to address specific areas of concern, ensuring a direct and impactful approach to healing.

Affirmations for Self-Discovery:

Pendulum Commands become affirmations for self-discovery. As readers pose commands, they unravel layers of the subconscious, gaining deeper insights into their thought patterns and emotional responses. The pendulum becomes a partner in the journey towards heightened self-awareness.

Breaking Chains of Limitation:

Specific attention is given to the transformative potential of Pendulum Commands in breaking chains of limitation. By directing commands towards dismantling self-imposed barriers, readers engage in a process of liberation. The pendulum, in this context, becomes a key to unlocking newfound freedom.

Energetic Alignment Through Commands:

The chapter explores how Pendulum Commands contribute to energetic alignment. By aligning thoughts and intentions through intentional commands, individuals foster a harmonious resonance between their conscious desires and subconscious beliefs. The pendulum becomes a guide in navigating this intricate dance of energies.

Transformation of Negative Patterns:

Pendulum Commands serve as instruments for the transformation of negative thought patterns. Readers learn to redirect energy through positive commands, interrupting and reshaping habitual negativity. The pendulum becomes a beacon of positivity, leading individuals towards a more constructive mindset.

Cultivating a Pendulum Ritual:

The incorporation of Pendulum Commands into a daily ritual is introduced as a powerful practice. By establishing a consistent dialogue with the pendulum, readers create a sacred space for intentional healing. The pendulum becomes not only a tool but a trusted companion in the journey towards wholeness.

Healing the Roots of Projection:

A significant aspect of this chapter is the exploration of how Pendulum Commands can heal the roots of projection. By addressing underlying beliefs and emotions through intentional language, individuals disrupt the cycle of projection at its source. The pendulum becomes a guide to the origins of projection, facilitating profound healing.

Case Studies of Command Efficacy:

Real-life case studies highlight the efficacy of Pendulum Commands in diverse scenarios. These narratives provide concrete examples of how individuals have successfully employed commands to dissolve projections and foster personal growth. The pendulum emerges as a reliable ally in their stories of transformation.

Empowerment as a Continuous Process:

The chapter concludes with the recognition that empowerment through Pendulum Commands is a continuous process. The pendulum becomes a companion on the ongoing journey of self-discovery and healing. Readers are encouraged to embrace the evolving nature of this empowerment, recognizing the pendulum as a timeless source of guidance.

"Remedies Through Pendulum Commands" stands as a testament to the transformative potential inherent in intentional language and the responsive guidance of the pendulum. As readers master the art of crafting and employing commands, they embark on a journey of profound healing, self-empowerment, and the dissolution of projections that hinder personal growth.

Chapter 6:

Balancing Energies

This chapter delves into the delicate balance of energies necessary for healing projections. Practical exercises guide readers in using the pendulum to assess and harmonize their energetic fields. The pendulum becomes a harmonizer, aiding individuals in restoring equilibrium and fostering a healthier relationship with themselves and others.

Harmonizing the Inner Symphony:

As the narrative unfolds into the realm of "Balancing Energies," readers are invited to explore the intricate dance of their internal energies. This chapter serves as a guide to harmonizing the symphony within, recognizing the interconnected rhythms of mind, body, and spirit.

Understanding Energetic Imbalances:

The chapter commences by shedding light on the concept of energetic imbalances. Readers gain insights into how disruptions in the flow of energy can manifest as physical, emotional, or mental challenges. The pendulum becomes a diagnostic tool, assisting individuals in identifying areas of imbalance.

Pendulum as an Energetic Harmonizer:

Central to this exploration is the revelation of the pendulum as an energetic harmonizer. Readers discover how the pendulum's movements can be utilized to assess and realign the subtle energies within the body. Practical exercises guide individuals in using the pendulum for chakra balancing and overall energetic equilibrium.

Chakra Alignment for Holistic Well-Being:

The chapter delves into the significance of chakra alignment in achieving holistic well-being. Through the guidance of the pendulum, readers learn to balance and activate their chakras, fostering a harmonious flow of energy. The pendulum becomes a key to unlocking vitality and promoting a sense of overall balance.

Pendulum Commands for Energy Alignment:

Building on the foundation of Pendulum Commands, the chapter introduces specific commands designed to align and balance energies. Readers engage in exercises that focus on intentional language to direct the pendulum in restoring equilibrium to areas of energetic imbalance. The pendulum emerges as a conductor orchestrating a harmonizing energy symphony.

Grounding Techniques for Stability:

Grounding techniques are unveiled as essential tools for stability and balance. Readers explore how the pendulum can be employed to facilitate grounding exercises, connecting individuals to the stabilizing energies of the earth. The pendulum becomes a bridge between the ethereal and the grounded, promoting a sense of centeredness.

Energetic Resonance with the Environment:

The exploration extends to the resonance between personal energies and the external environment. Readers learn to use the pendulum to assess and attune their energies to the energies of their surroundings. This awareness empowers individuals to navigate life with a heightened sensitivity to energetic influences.

Maintaining Balance in Daily Life:

Practical tips and exercises guide readers in maintaining energetic balance in their daily lives. The pendulum becomes a constant companion, offering guidance on how to navigate the challenges and demands of life while preserving a state of internal equilibrium. This integration transforms the pendulum from a therapeutic tool into a lifestyle ally.

Energetic Hygiene for Emotional Well-Being:

The chapter emphasizes the importance of energetic hygiene for emotional well-being. Readers explore how the pendulum can be utilized for clearing stagnant energies, releasing emotional residues, and fostering a state of emotional clarity. The pendulum becomes a tool for maintaining a clean and vibrant energy field.

Self-Care Rituals Through Energetic Awareness:

The chapter concludes by encouraging readers to develop self-care rituals rooted in energetic awareness. The pendulum becomes a guide in crafting personalized rituals that nourish the mind, body, and spirit. Readers are empowered to take an active role in their well-being through the integration of intentional practices.

In "Balancing Energies," readers embark on a transformative journey of aligning with the harmonious rhythms of their internal energies. The pendulum, as a conductor in this symphony, guides individuals towards a state of equilibrium, resilience, and vibrant well-being.

Chapter 7:

Pendulum Healing for Interpersonal Relationships

Expanding the focus, this chapter explores how Pendulum Healing can be applied to interpersonal relationships affected by projections. Readers gain insights into using the pendulum to navigate conflicts, improve communication, and foster understanding. The pendulum becomes a mediator, facilitating healing and harmony in relationships.

Navigating the Energetic Web of Relationships:

The narrative unfolds into the rich tapestry of interpersonal dynamics in "Pendulum Healing for Interpersonal Relationships." Readers embark on a profound exploration of how the pendulum becomes a healing catalyst, offering insights and remedies to enhance the energetic connections between individuals.

The Pendulum as a Relationship Guide:

Central to this chapter is the recognition of the pendulum as a relationship guide. Readers discover how the pendulum can be utilized to assess and navigate the subtle energies between individuals. It becomes a tool for unraveling the complexities of relationships and fostering a deeper understanding of the energetic exchanges at play.

Assessing Energetic Compatibility:

Practical exercises guide readers in using the pendulum to assess energetic compatibility in relationships. By posing targeted questions, individuals gain insights into the alignment of energies, values, and communication styles. The pendulum becomes a discerning ally, offering clarity on the dynamics that contribute to harmonious connections.

Resolving Energetic Tensions:

The chapter delves into how the pendulum serves as a mediator in resolving energetic tensions. Readers explore techniques for identifying and addressing energetic imbalances that may lead to conflicts or misunderstandings. The pendulum becomes a bridge for open communication and mutual understanding.

Pendulum Commands for Relationship Harmony:

Building on the concept of Pendulum Commands, readers engage in exercises focused on fostering relationship harmony. Intentional commands become tools for dissolving negative energies, promoting empathy, and nurturing a positive energetic environment. The pendulum becomes a conduit for co-creating a shared energetic space.

Energetic Boundaries and Empathy:

The exploration extends to the importance of establishing energetic boundaries and cultivating empathy. Readers learn how the pendulum can be utilized to assess and strengthen energetic boundaries, fostering a healthy balance between individual and shared energies. The pendulum becomes a guide in developing empathetic connections within relationships.

Healing Past Energetic Residue:

The chapter addresses the impact of past energetic residue on present relationships. Readers explore how the pendulum can assist in identifying and healing unresolved energies from previous interactions. It becomes a transformative tool for releasing old patterns and creating a foundation for renewed connections.

Energetic Alignment in Communication:

Practical insights guide readers in using the pendulum to enhance energetic alignment in communication. By posing questions related to effective communication, individuals gain clarity on how to convey their thoughts and emotions in a way that resonates energetically. The pendulum becomes a facilitator for clear and harmonious expression.

Pendulum Rituals for Relationship Maintenance:

Readers are encouraged to incorporate pendulum rituals into their relationship maintenance practices. The chapter introduces personalized rituals that utilize the pendulum for checking in on energetic well-being, expressing gratitude, and fostering a continuous flow of positive energy within relationships.

Cultivating a Relationship-Positive Mindset:

The chapter concludes by emphasizing the cultivation of a relationship-positive mindset. Readers explore how the pendulum can be a tool for shifting perspectives, promoting forgiveness, and fostering a mindset that contributes to the growth and evolution of interpersonal connections.

In "Pendulum Healing for Interpersonal Relationships," the pendulum becomes a guiding light in the intricate dance of connections. This chapter empowers readers to cultivate energetically harmonious relationships, fostering a depth of understanding and mutual growth within the shared energetic space.

Chapter 8:

Advanced Pendulum Techniques

For those ready to deepen their Pendulum Healing practice, this chapter introduces advanced techniques. From chakra balancing to past-life regressions, the pendulum becomes a versatile instrument for profound self-exploration and healing. Practical exercises provide guidance for readers eager to expand their pendulum expertise.

Unlocking Deeper Realms of Possibility:

In the culmination of the pendulum journey, "Advanced Pendulum Techniques" invites readers to explore the far-reaching capabilities of this ancient tool. This chapter delves into advanced methodologies, pushing the boundaries of traditional pendulum use and unveiling the potential for profound transformation.

Quantum Pendulum Concepts:

Readers are introduced to quantum pendulum concepts, elevating the understanding of the pendulum's responsiveness. The chapter explores how quantum principles can be applied to enhance the accuracy and depth of pendulum responses. The pendulum becomes a quantum oracle, tapping into realms beyond conventional perception.

Multidimensional Exploration with the Pendulum:

The exploration extends into the realm of multidimensional energies. Readers embark on a journey of using the pendulum to access and navigate various dimensions of consciousness. This advanced technique opens doors to expanded states of awareness, offering insights that transcend the limitations of everyday perception.

Intuitive Pendulum Programming:

The chapter unveils intuitive pendulum programming as a technique for imbuing the pendulum with personalized energetic signatures. Readers learn how to intuitively program the pendulum to align with specific energies, intentions, or entities. The pendulum transforms into a customized instrument for intricate energetic work.

Time-Traveling with the Pendulum:

A bold exploration unfolds as readers discover the potential for time-traveling with the pendulum. This advanced technique allows individuals to access information from past or future timelines. The pendulum becomes a bridge through the fabric of time, offering glimpses into events, insights, and possibilities beyond the present moment.

Parallel Realities and Decision-Making:

The chapter delves into the concept of parallel realities and how the pendulum can be employed for decision-making across multiple timelines. Readers explore techniques for seeking guidance on choices and actions that align with their highest potentials across different branches of existence. The pendulum becomes a compass in navigating the vast landscape of possibilities.

Morphic Resonance and Energetic Imprinting:

Advanced pendulum techniques include an exploration of morphic resonance and energetic imprinting. Readers learn how to tap into the collective field of information and imprint specific energies onto objects or spaces. The pendulum becomes a tool for creating intentional energetic imprints that influence environments and experiences.

Remote Viewing and Energetic Projection:

The chapter unveils techniques for remote viewing and energetic projection using the pendulum. Readers explore how the pendulum can be utilized as a tool for perceiving and influencing distant locations or situations. This advanced application expands the scope of pendulum work to transcend physical boundaries.

Pendulum Healing Circles:

Readers are introduced to the concept of pendulum healing circles, where multiple individuals join forces to amplify healing energies. The chapter provides guidance on how to create and participate in group pendulum sessions for collective healing and intention manifestation. The pendulum becomes a focal point for shared energetic intentions.

Ethical Considerations in Advanced Pendulum Work:

The exploration concludes with a discussion on ethical considerations in advanced pendulum work. Readers are guided on responsible and respectful practices, ensuring that the application of advanced techniques aligns with principles of integrity, consent, and well-being. The pendulum becomes not only a tool of empowerment but also a beacon of ethical exploration.

In "Advanced Pendulum Techniques," readers transcend the conventional boundaries of pendulum use, stepping into the realm of limitless possibilities. The pendulum, as an advanced guide, becomes a key to unlocking mysteries, expanding consciousness, and exploring the frontiers of energetic exploration.

Chapter 9:

Integration and Empowerment

The concluding chapter weaves together the threads of knowledge and healing. Readers are guided through a process of integrating newfound awareness and empowerment into their daily lives. The pendulum emerges as a lifelong companion, a source of ongoing guidance and support on the journey to self-discovery and transformation.

Harvesting the Fruits of the Pendulum Journey:

As the pendulum journey nears its culmination, "Integration and Empowerment" serves as the bridge between newfound wisdom and transformative empowerment. Readers are guided in the integration of pendulum practices into their lives, fostering a continuous journey of self-discovery and empowerment.

Reflecting on the Pendulum Journey:

The chapter commences with a reflective exploration of the pendulum journey. Readers are encouraged to revisit key insights, experiences, and transformations that have unfolded throughout the chapters. The pendulum becomes a reflective tool, illuminating the progress made and the seeds of potential yet to be sown.

Creating Personal Pendulum Rituals:

Practical guidance is offered on creating personalized pendulum rituals. Readers are empowered to establish rituals that align with their preferences, schedules, and intentions. The pendulum becomes an integral part of daily or weekly routines, offering a consistent source of guidance and empowerment.

Incorporating Pendulum Insights into Decision-Making:

Readers learn how to integrate pendulum insights into their decision-making processes. The chapter provides techniques for posing targeted questions to the pendulum when faced with choices. The pendulum becomes a trusted advisor, offering clarity and alignment with one's higher purpose in decision-making.

Elevating Personal Energy with Pendulum Practices:

The pendulum is harnessed as a tool for elevating personal energy. Readers explore techniques for using the pendulum to clear energetic blockages, balance chakras, and enhance overall vitality. The pendulum becomes a source of revitalization, promoting a heightened sense of well-being.

Empowering Affirmations and Pendulum Commands:

The integration extends to the empowerment of affirmations and Pendulum Commands. Readers discover how to craft personalized affirmations and commands that align with their evolving goals and aspirations. The pendulum becomes a catalyst for manifesting positive change through intentional language.

Continuous Learning and Adaptation:

The chapter emphasizes the importance of continuous learning and adaptation in the realm of pendulum practices. Readers are encouraged to explore new techniques, experiment with advanced concepts, and adapt their approaches based on evolving insights. The pendulum becomes a dynamic companion in the ever-unfolding journey of personal growth.

Sharing Pendulum Wisdom with Others:

Readers are invited to share their pendulum wisdom with others. Whether through facilitating pendulum workshops, engaging in group sessions, or simply introducing friends and family to pendulum practices, individuals become ambassadors of empowerment. The pendulum's influence ripples outward, contributing to collective well-being.

Pendulum as a Symbol of Empowerment:

The chapter concludes by highlighting the pendulum as a symbol of personal empowerment. Readers are encouraged to view the pendulum not just as a divination tool but as a representation of their inner strength, intuition, and capacity for positive change. The pendulum becomes a talisman, a tangible reminder of their journey towards empowerment.

In "Integration and Empowerment," readers merge the insights gained from the pendulum journey into the fabric of their lives. The pendulum, having served as a guide, mentor, and catalyst for transformation, becomes an enduring companion in the ongoing narrative of self-discovery and empowerment.

"Projection to Empowerment" serves as a comprehensive guide for those seeking to unravel the complexities of psychological projections and harness the healing power of Pendulum Therapy. Through insightful exploration, practical exercises, and transformative remedies, this book invites readers to embark on a journey of self-discovery, empowerment, and holistic healing.

When using a pendulum for reducing projections and improving accuracy in pendulum work, incorporating specific commands or affirmations can help align your mindset and focus. Here are some commands or affirmations you can use before and during a pendulum session to reduce projections:

1. "I Am Open to Receiving Clear and Unbiased Answers": This affirmation sets the intention to receive information without personal biases or expectations.

2. "May Only the Highest Truth and Guidance Come Through": Setting the intention to receive guidance from a higher source, free from personal influences.

3. "I Release All Personal Biases and Expectations": Acknowledging and releasing any preconceived notions or desires that might impact the pendulum's movement.

4. "Grant Me Clarity and Objectivity in This Session": Seeking mental clarity and an objective perspective during the session.

5. "I Connect to Pure, Unadulterated Energy for Accurate Readings": Establishing a connection to a clear, pure source of energy for accurate pendulum readings.

6. "May the Pendulum Reflect Truth Beyond My Personal Interpretation": Encouraging the pendulum to reflect objective truths rather than subjective interpretation.

7. "I Ground Myself and Remain Centered for Clear Communication": Grounding and centering oneself to enhance focus and reduce emotional influence on the pendulum's movement.

8. "I Trust the Divine Wisdom and Guidance to Flow Freely": Opening up to trust in a higher wisdom or universal guidance during the pendulum session. Remember to speak these commands or affirmations aloud or mentally while holding the pendulum and setting your intentions. The goal is to create a clear, receptive, and

neutral state of mind for accurate and unbiased readings, reducing the influence of personal projections on the pendulum's movement.

9. "I Release Ego and Embrace Objectivity": Acknowledging and releasing the influence of ego, allowing for a more objective interpretation of the pendulum's movement.

10. "Grant Me the Wisdom to Interpret Answers Without Bias": Seeking wisdom to interpret the pendulum's responses objectively and without personal bias.

11. "May Only Clear and Pure Energy Influence This Session": Invoking clear, pure energy to guide the pendulum and reduce personal influence.

12. "I Embrace Detachment and Allow Answers to Flow Unhindered": Embracing a sense of detachment from desired outcomes, allowing the pendulum to move freely.

13. "I Welcome Insights Aligned with Highest Good": Inviting insights that are aligned with the greater good and not influenced by personal desires or attachments.

14. "I Ground My Energy and Maintain a Calm State of Mind": Grounding oneself in a calm, centered state of mind to minimize the impact of emotions on the pendulum's movement.

15. "Grant Clarity and Accuracy in Each Response": Seeking clear and accurate responses from the pendulum, enhancing the focus on precision and clarity.

16. "I Release Control and Surrender to the Wisdom of the Pendulum": Letting go of the need to control the pendulum and surrendering to its wisdom for guidance.

17. "May My Mind, Heart, and Spirit Align for Unbiased Answers": Seeking alignment between mind, heart, and spirit to receive unbiased and accurate information.

18. "I Accept and Respect the Limitations of Pendulum Guidance": Recognizing and respecting the boundaries and limitations of the pendulum's guidance while seeking to reduce personal influence.

Employ these commands or affirmations as part of your pre-session preparation or during the session to set the tone and intention for a more objective, accurate, and less influenced experience with the pendulum. Combining these affirmations with self-awareness and a clear, receptive mindset can help minimize personal projections in pendulum work.

19. "May My Intentions Align with Truth and Clarity": Seeking alignment between personal intentions and the quest for truth and clarity in the pendulum's movements.

20. "I Invoke Higher Guidance Beyond Personal Influences": Calling upon higher guidance, such as universal wisdom or spiritual sources, to guide the pendulum independently of personal influences.

21. "Grant Me the Wisdom to Distinguish Between Truth and Projection": Requesting the discernment needed to differentiate between genuine responses and personal projections.

22. "I Embrace Patience and Trust in the Process": Encouraging patience and trust in the unfolding process of receiving accurate information while minimizing personal haste or impatience.

23. "I Connect to Pure, Unbiased Energy for Clear Communication": Establishing a connection to untainted energy sources to facilitate clear communication and interpretation.

24. "I Reaffirm Neutrality in Mind, Body, and Spirit": Reaffirming the need for neutrality in thoughts, actions, and spirit to receive unbiased and accurate information.

25. "May Each Movement Reflect Universal Truth and Clarity": Invoking universal truths and clarity in every movement of the pendulum to reduce personal influences.

26. "I Maintain Honesty and Openness to Genuine Responses": Committing to honesty and openness to receive genuine responses from the pendulum without manipulation.

27. "I Cultivate Self-Awareness to Minimize Personal Biases": Fostering self-awareness to recognize and reduce personal biases during pendulum sessions.

28. "May the Pendulum Reflect Only What Serves My Highest Good": Requesting guidance that aligns with personal growth, highest good, and the well-being of all involved.

Using these commands in conjunction with a calm, focused mindset and an intention for objectivity can significantly reduce the impact of personal projections and biases, allowing for clearer and more accurate pendulum readings. Remember, regular practice, selfreflection, and ongoing self-improvement contribute to refining the accuracy of pendulum work over time.

29. "I Release Fear and Doubt, Inviting Certainty and Clarity": Letting go of fear and doubt that might cloud the mind and invite certainty and clarity during the session.

30. "I Set Aside Expectations for Unbiased Insights": Putting aside personal expectations and desires, allowing the pendulum to provide insights without influence.

31. "I Trust in the Pendulum's Objective Guidance": Building trust in the pendulum's ability to offer objective guidance independent of personal influence.

32. "May Each Response Reflect Unfiltered Truth": Requesting that each movement or response of the pendulum reflect pure, unfiltered truth.

33. "I Release Attachment to Specific Outcomes": Detaching from specific outcomes or desires, allowing the pendulum to move freely without being influenced by personal wishes.

34. "I Cultivate a State of Mental Clarity and Focus": Fostering a state of mental clarity and unwavering focus during the pendulum session to ensure accuracy.

35. "I Embrace Equanimity to Receive Unbiased Information": Welcoming a state of equanimity, enabling the receipt of information without prejudice or bias.

36. "I Integrate Self-Reflection to Enhance Accuracy": Incorporating regular self-reflection to improve accuracy by understanding personal patterns and influences.

37. "May My Mind and Heart Align for Clear Interpretation": Aligning both rational thought and emotional understanding to interpret the pendulum's movements accurately.

38. "I Seek Harmony Between Intuition and Rationality": Striving for a balance between intuitive insights and rational thinking for accurate interpretations.

By incorporating these commands and practices into your pendulum sessions, you can create a conducive environment for reducing projections and enhancing the accuracy of the pendulum's responses. Remember that personal growth and self-awareness play crucial roles in refining your ability to work with the pendulum effectively.

39. "I Invoke Clarity and Harmony in Energy Alignment": Inviting a harmonious alignment of energies, fostering clarity and reducing personal interference in the pendulum's movements.

40. "May My Intentions Align with Universal Truth": Setting intentions to synchronize personal motives with universal truths for unbiased responses.

41. "I Seek Guidance from the Purest Source of Wisdom": Calling upon the purest source of wisdom to guide the pendulum's movements beyond personal influence.

42. "I Ground Myself in the Present Moment for Clear Readings": Staying grounded in the present moment to ensure clear and accurate readings from the pendulum.

43. "I Acknowledge and Release Limiting Beliefs Affecting Readings": Acknowledging and releasing any limiting beliefs that might influence the pendulum's responses.

44. "I Connect with Higher Consciousness for Unbiased Interpretation": Establishing a connection with higher consciousness to aid in interpreting responses without bias.

45. "I Embrace Detachment to Allow Unhindered Insight": Embracing a state of detachment to allow insights to flow freely without personal interference.

46. "I Invoke Gratitude for the Clarity and Accuracy Received": Expressing gratitude for the clarity and accuracy received from the pendulum, reinforcing the intention for unbiased responses.

47. "May Every Movement Reflect Universal Wisdom": Requesting that each movement of the pendulum is guided by universal wisdom, transcending personal projections.

48. "I Cultivate Humility and Openness for Clearer Understanding": Embracing humility and openness to foster a clearer understanding of the pendulum's guidance.

Utilize these commands and practices to enhance your pendulum work by reducing personal projections and biases. Remember, practice, self-awareness, and a commitment to personal growth are fundamental in refining your skills in using the pendulum as a tool for guidance and insight

End.